Mel Bay and Warner Bros. Publications Present...

Fingerstyle JAZZ

The "La Cremona Fiorita" guitar used on the front and back covers appears courtesy of Robert Benedetto.
The front cover photo by Ronald Chicken, back cover photo by Skot Koenig.

1 2 3 4 5 6 7 8 9 0

Visit us on the Web at www.melbay.com — E-mail us at email@melbay.com

Contents

Many arrangers were used for the completion of this project. Therefore, there is no standardized nomenclature for all the chords and their embellishments. For example, an F/A may be written above a chord that has the notes F, A, C, and G. This is an Fadd9 chord, but functions as an F chord. This will help students see, in some cases, how chord embellishments relate to a parent chord.

ALL THE THINGS YOU ARE

Arr: CRAIG WAGNER

Music by JEROME KERN
Words by OSCAR HAMMERSTEIN II

4

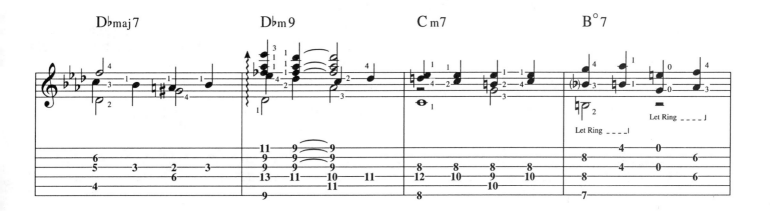

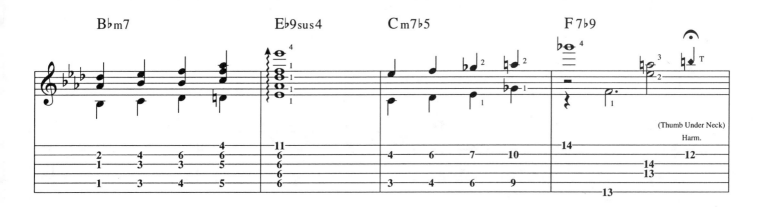

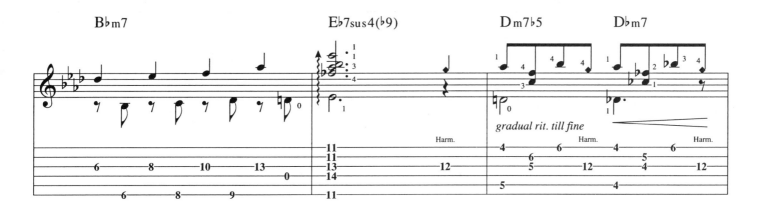

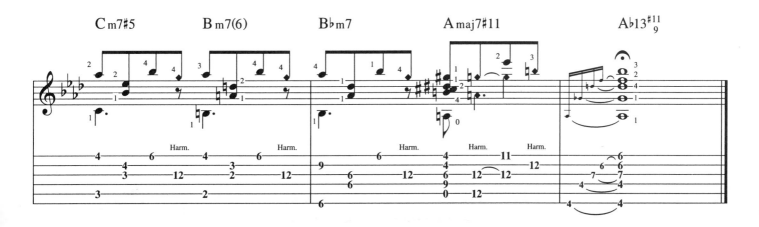

Alone Together

Arr: DAVE BLACK

Words by HOWARD DIETZ
Music by ARTHUR SCHWARTZ

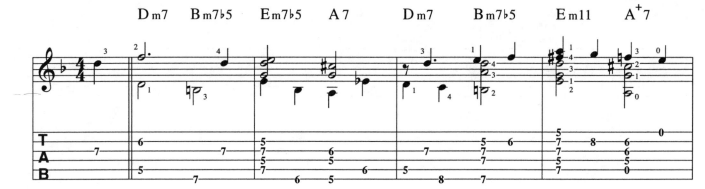

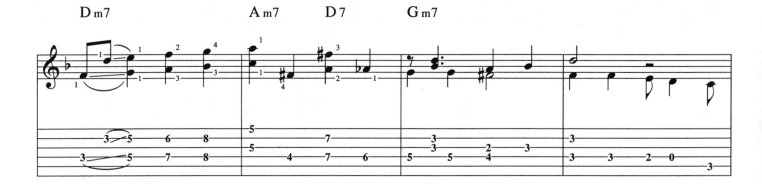

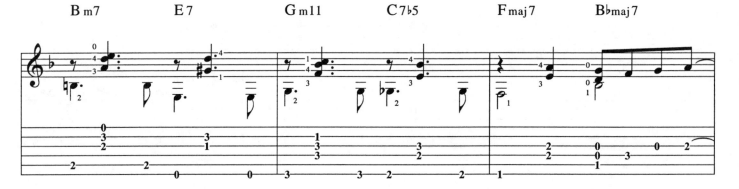

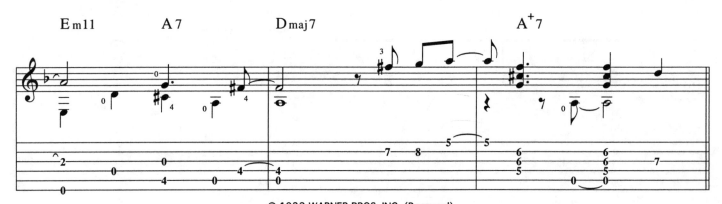

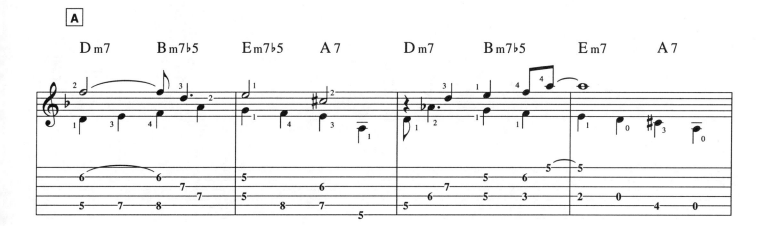

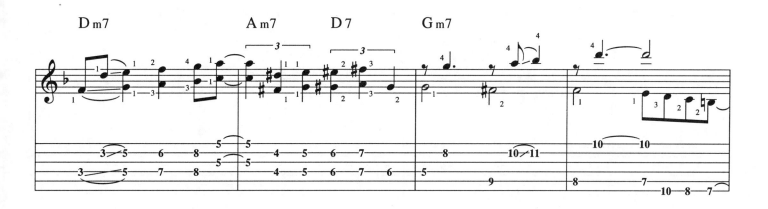

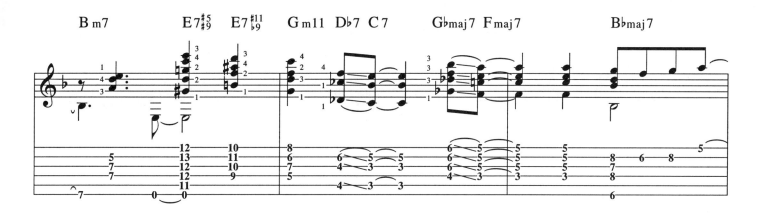

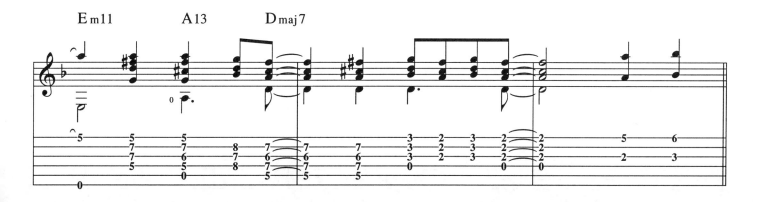

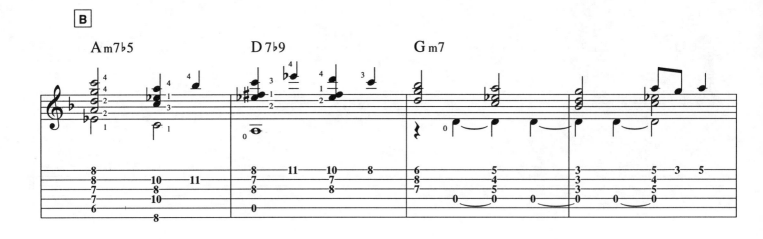

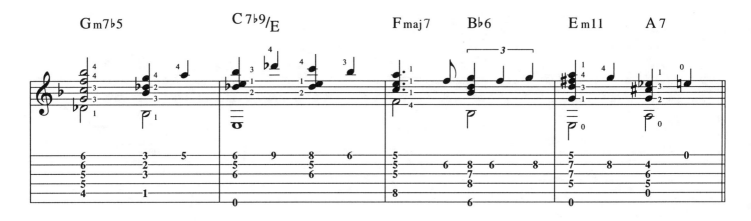

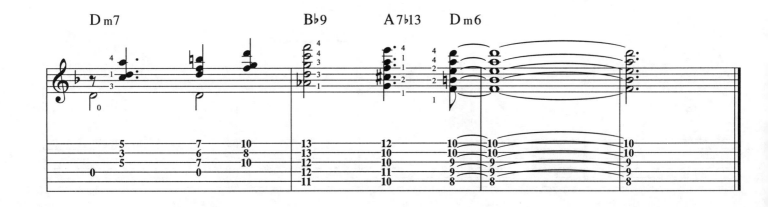

BEAUTIFUL LOVE

Arr: CHRIS BUZZELLI

Words and Music by
VICTOR YOUNG, WAYNE KING,
EGBERT VAN ALSTYNE
and HAVEN GILLESPIE

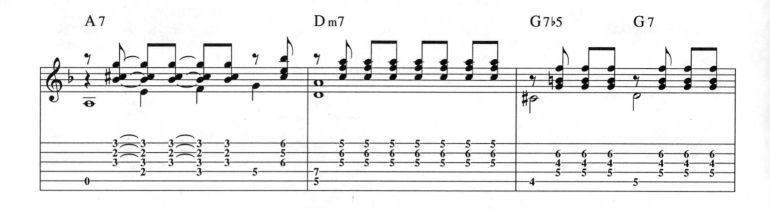

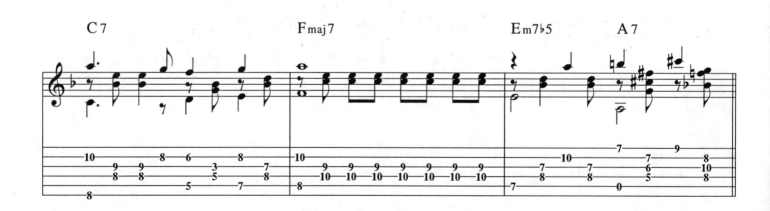

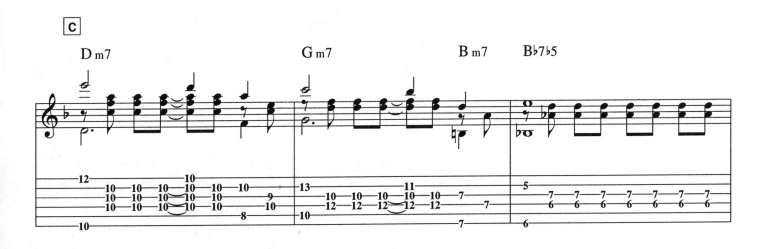

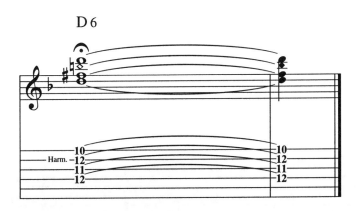

A Day in the Life of a Fool
(Manha de Carnaval)

Arr: CRAIG WAGNER

Words by CARL SIGMAN
Music by LUIZ BONFA

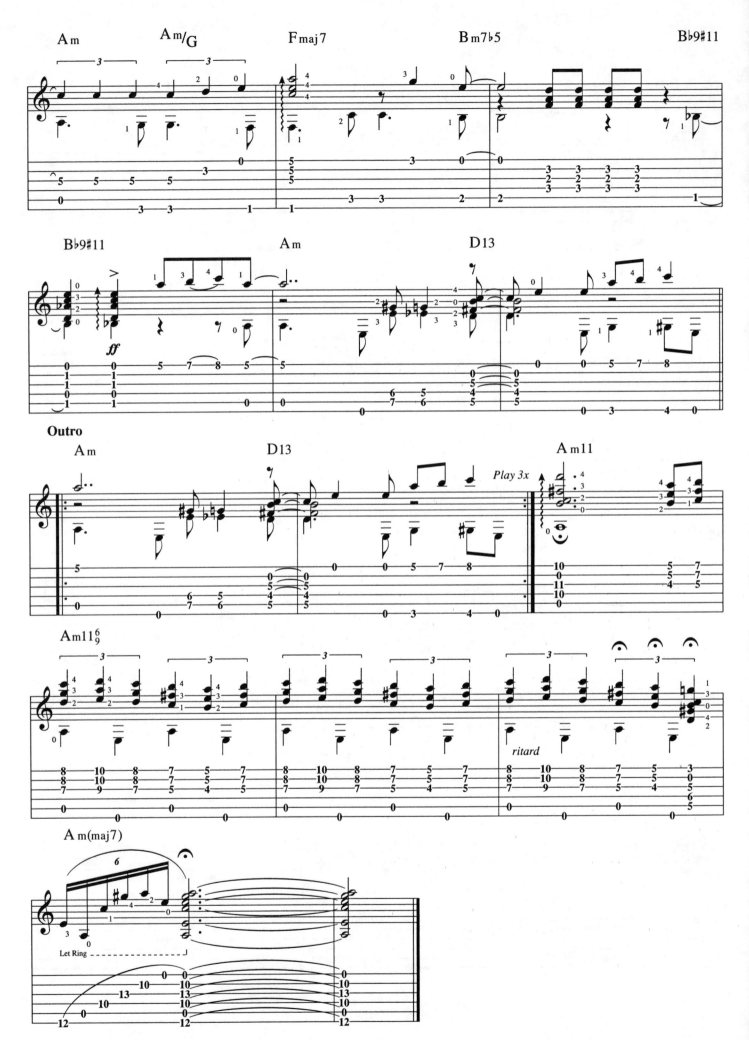

A FELICIDADE
(a/k/a Adieu Tristesse)

Arr: ALAN de MAUSE

Words and Music by
VINCIUS DE MORAES,
ANDRE SALVET and
ANTONIO CARLOS JOBIM

Intro

Medium Bossa

15

16

HAVE YOU MET MISS JONES?

Arr: CHRIS BUZZELLI

Words by LORENZ HART
Music by RICHARD RODGERS

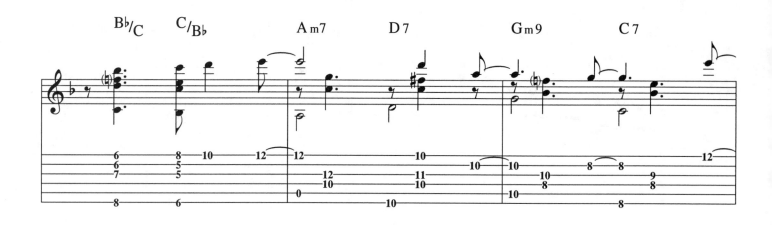

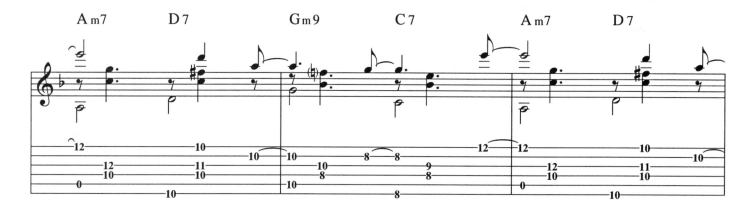

How High the Moon

Arr: DAVE BLACK

Words by NANCY HAMILTON
Music by MORGAN LEWIS

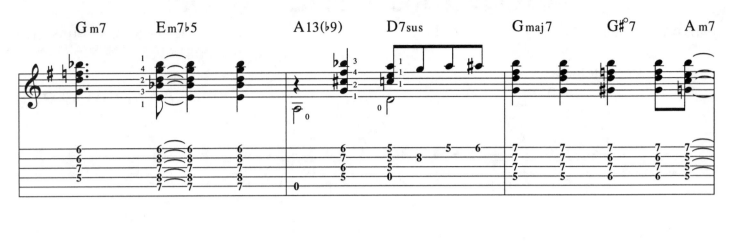

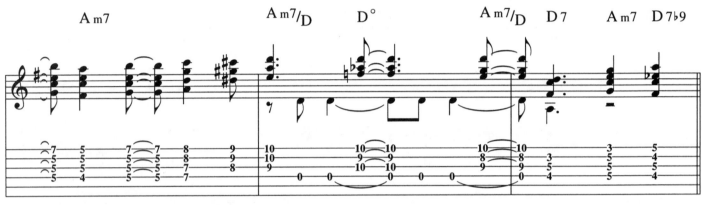

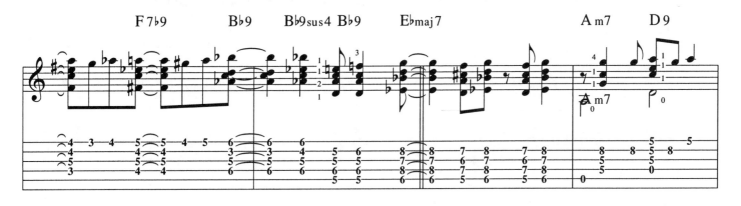

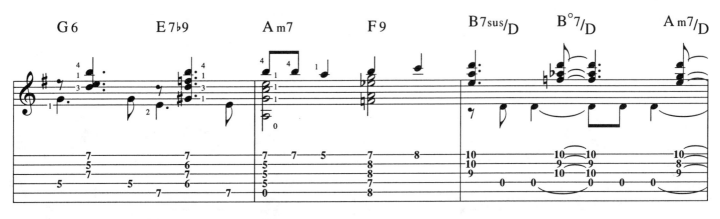

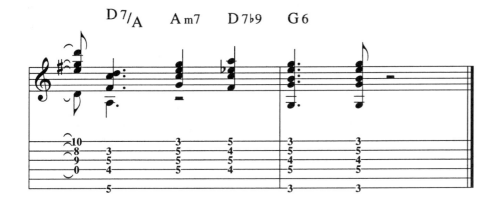

I Could Write A Book

Arr: CHRIS BUZZELLI

Words by LORENZ HART
Music by RICHARD RODGERS

I Love You

Arr: CRAIG WAGNER

Words and Music by
COLE PORTER

26

27

I'VE GOT YOU UNDER MY SKIN

Arr: DAVE BLACK

Words and Music by
COLE PORTER

JUST FRIENDS

Arr: RICHARD MAXWELL

Music by JOHN KLENNER
Lyric by SAM M. LEWIS

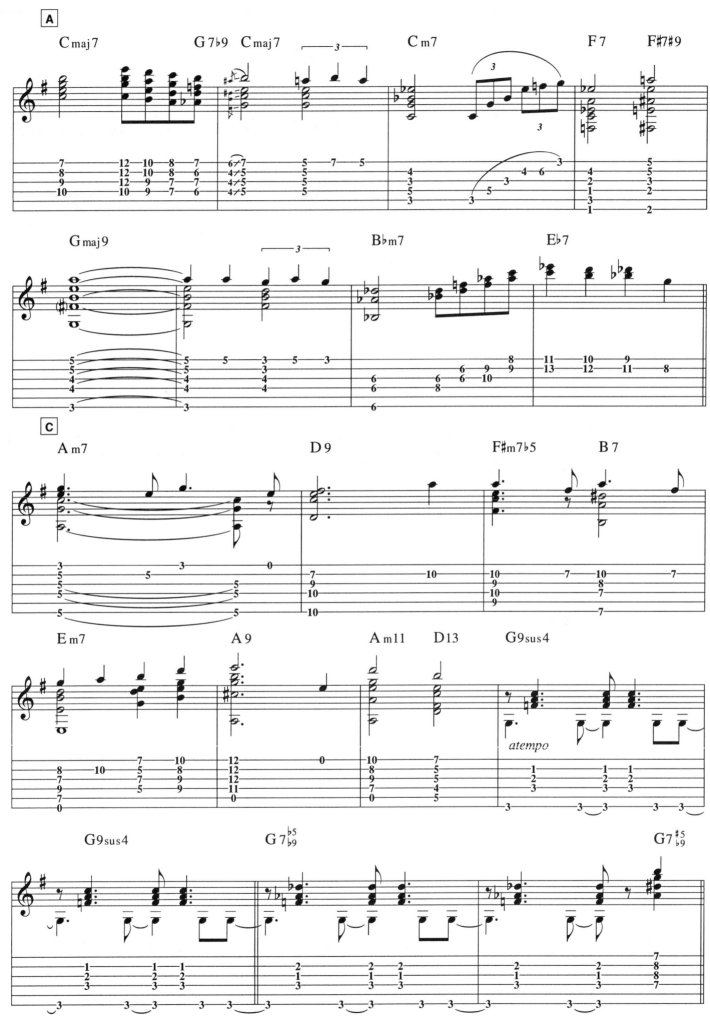

Makin' Whoopee

Arr: DAVE BLACK

Lyrics by GUS KAHN
Music by WALTER DONALDSON

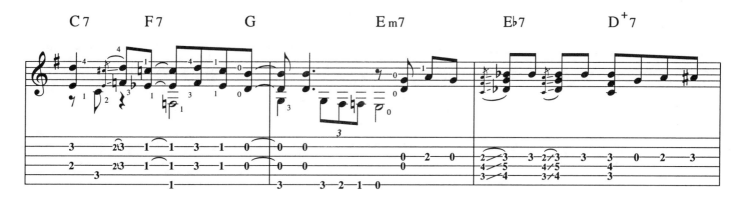

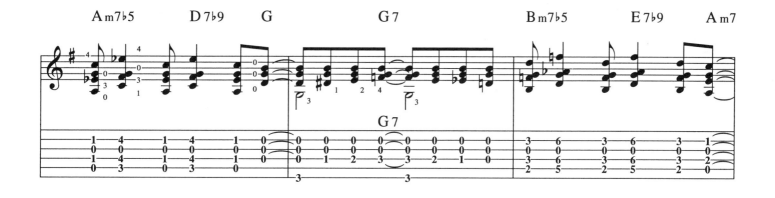

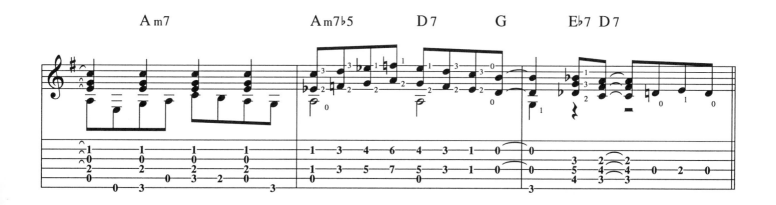

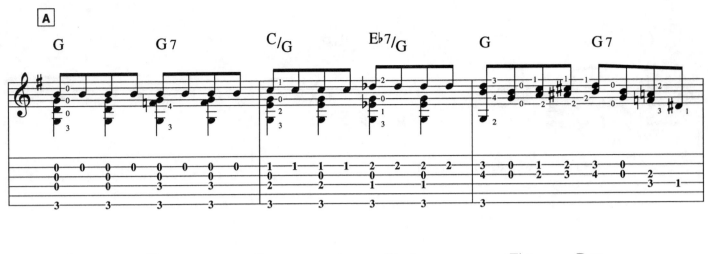

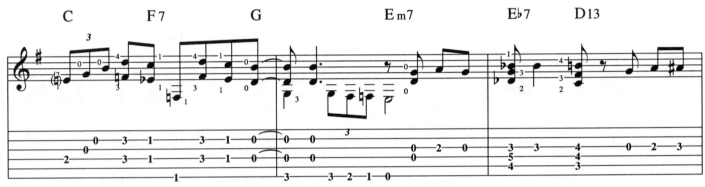

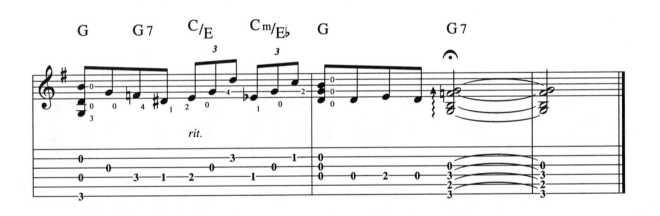

*This page has been
left blank to avoid
awkward page turns*

MY FUNNY VALENTINE

Arr: JERRY SIMS

Words by LORENZ HART
Music by RICHARD RODGERS

Secret Love

Arr: JERRY SIMS

Words by PAUL FRANCIS WEBSTER
Music by SAMMY FAIN

44

THE SHADOW OF YOUR SMILE

Arr: ALAN de MAUSE

Music by JOHNNY MANDEL
Words by PAUL FRANCIS WEBSTER

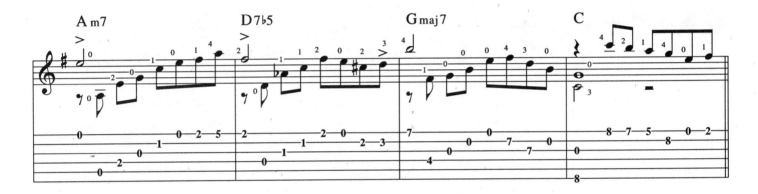

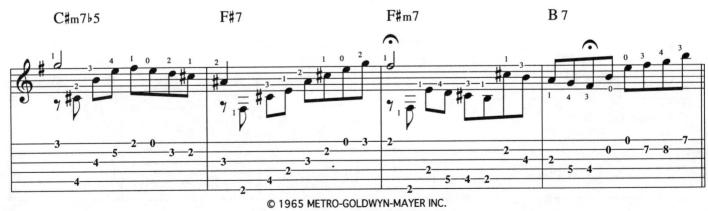

Summertime
(From Porgy and Bess®)

By GEORGE GERSHWIN, DuBOSE
AND DOROTHY HEYWARD
and IRA GERSHWIN

Arr: CRAIG WAGNER

B

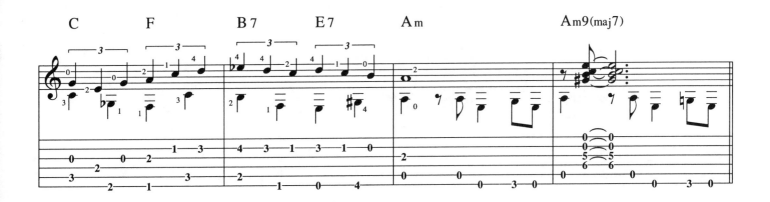

Interlude

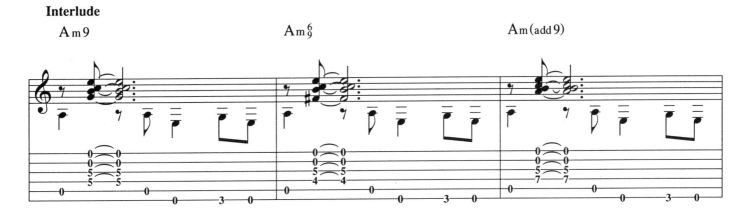

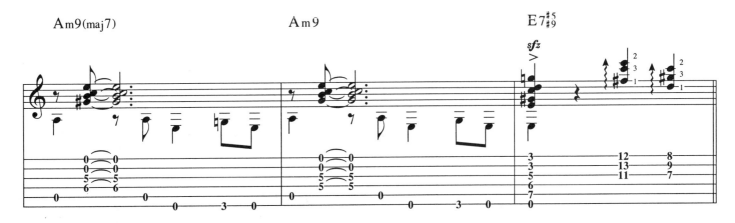

50

Outro

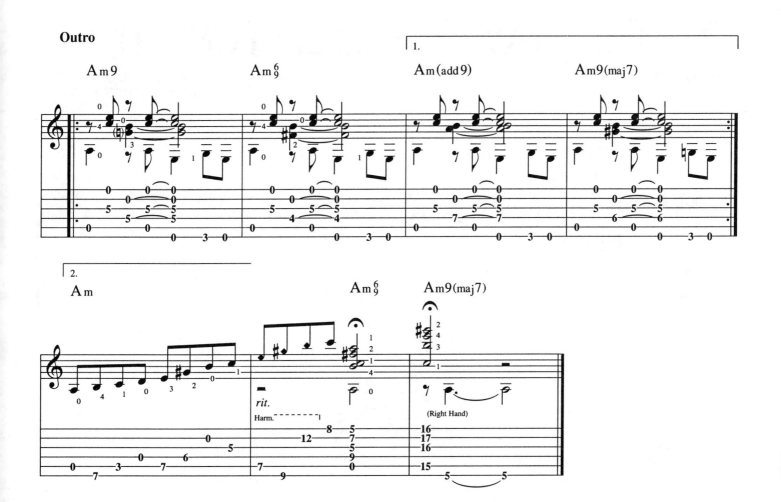

THE WAY YOU LOOK TONIGHT

Arr: CRAIG WAGNER

Music by JEROME KERN
Words by DOROTHY FIELDS

52

Interlude

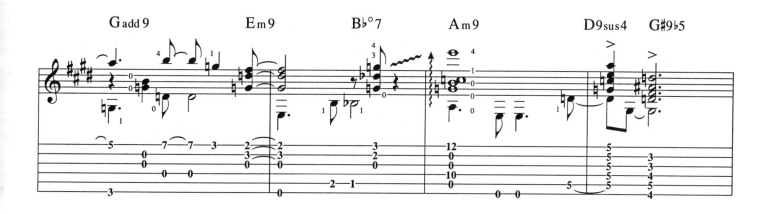

D.S. al Coda

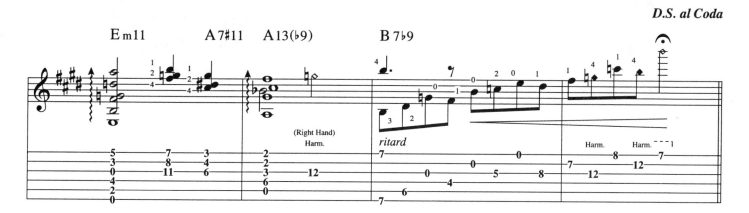

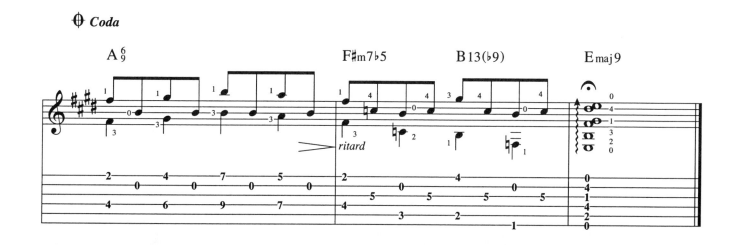